Chobham

N. W. SURREY
10 TOWN AND
COUNTRY RAMBLES

Written and illustrated by
Chris. Howkins

Mapwork by
Darren Hemsley

WRITTEN AND ILLUSTRATED
Chris Howkins

MAPWORK
Darren Hemsley

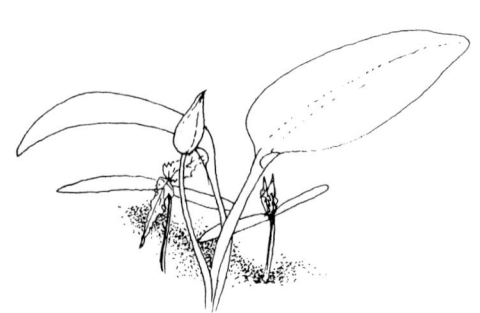

COPYRIGHT
Chris Howkins ©

FIRST EDITION 1989
Reprinted   1992

PUBLISHED
Chris Howkins,
70, Grange Road,
New Haw,
WEYBRIDGE,
Surrey, KT15 3RH.

PRINTED
Unwin Brothers Limited,
The Gresham Press,
OLD WOKING,
Surrey, England.
GU22 9LH.

2.

CONTENTS

INTRODUCTION

There's a great richness of beauty and social history in N.W. Surrey, enhanced by a wealth of wildlife. It's certainly not a concrete jungle. It's a matter of knowing where to look and what to look for.

With this in mind these route have been compiled to provide some starting points. They've been kept short to allow time to stop and look, time to wait for wildlife to show itself, time to wander off-course and explore further. Only in this way can the area be appreciated fully, as there's only room for brief notes in this little guide.

EASY WHEELING

Half of the routes have been chosen for being accessible to wheelchairs and pushchairs. The others will depend upon your strength and determination but as a guide : Chobham's churchyard gate may cause a problem but can be avoided; Cobham's ramble has deep sand and is steep but there's a surfaced path to Boldermere; Ottershaw's knoll is a steep rough climb but not if approached from the Chobham Road; Stonehill's tracks are very stony and the ramble over Weybridge's meadows involves crossing two railway embankments.

WARNING - The inclusion of a path in this book is no indication that it is a Public Right of Way.

LOCATION MAP of the Rambles

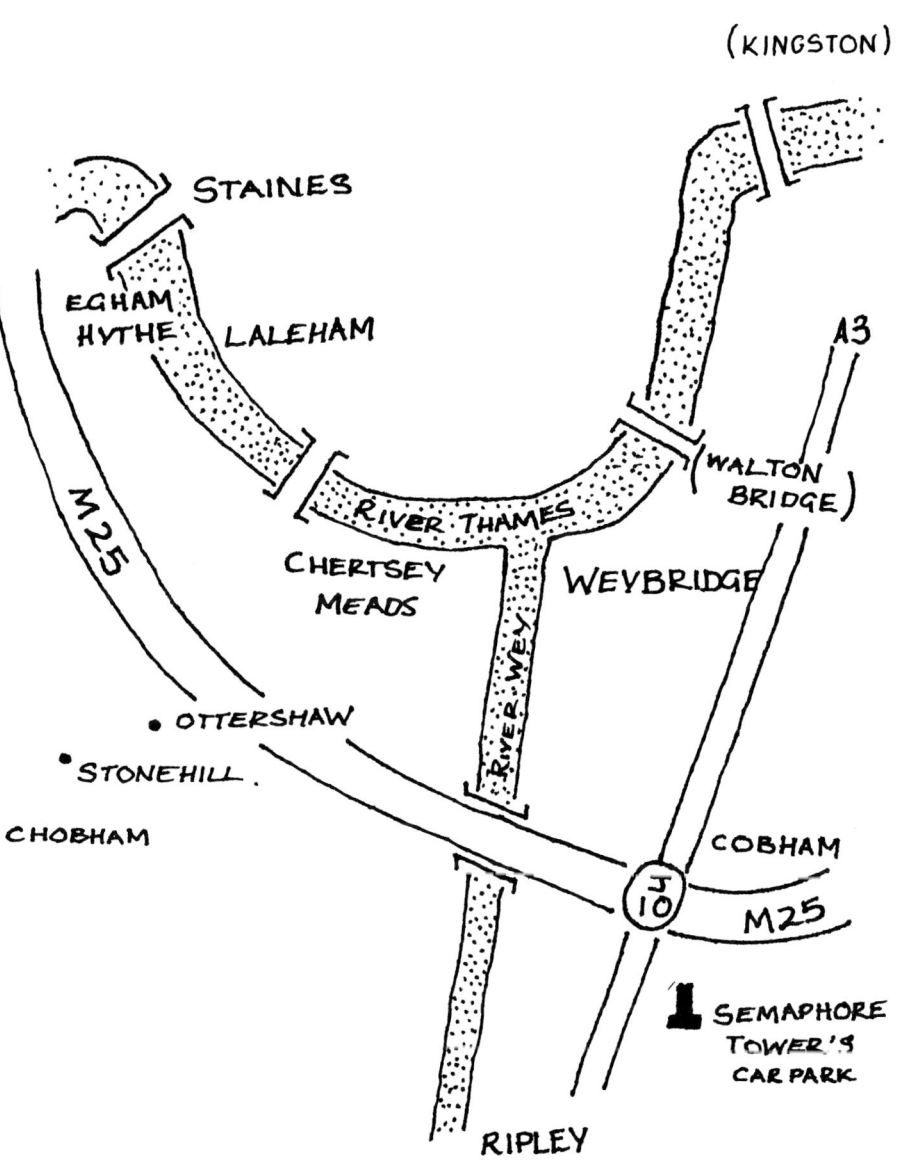

(KINGSTON)

STAINES

EGHAM HYTHE   LALEHAM

A3

M25

RIVER THAMES

WALTON BRIDGE

CHERTSEY MEADS   WEYBRIDGE

RIVER WEY

• OTTERSHAW

• STONEHILL

CHOBHAM

COBHAM

J 10   M25

SEMAPHORE TOWER'S CAR PARK

RIPLEY

5.

CHERTSEY MEADS : Wide Open Spaces

Distance : 2 miles or wander at will.

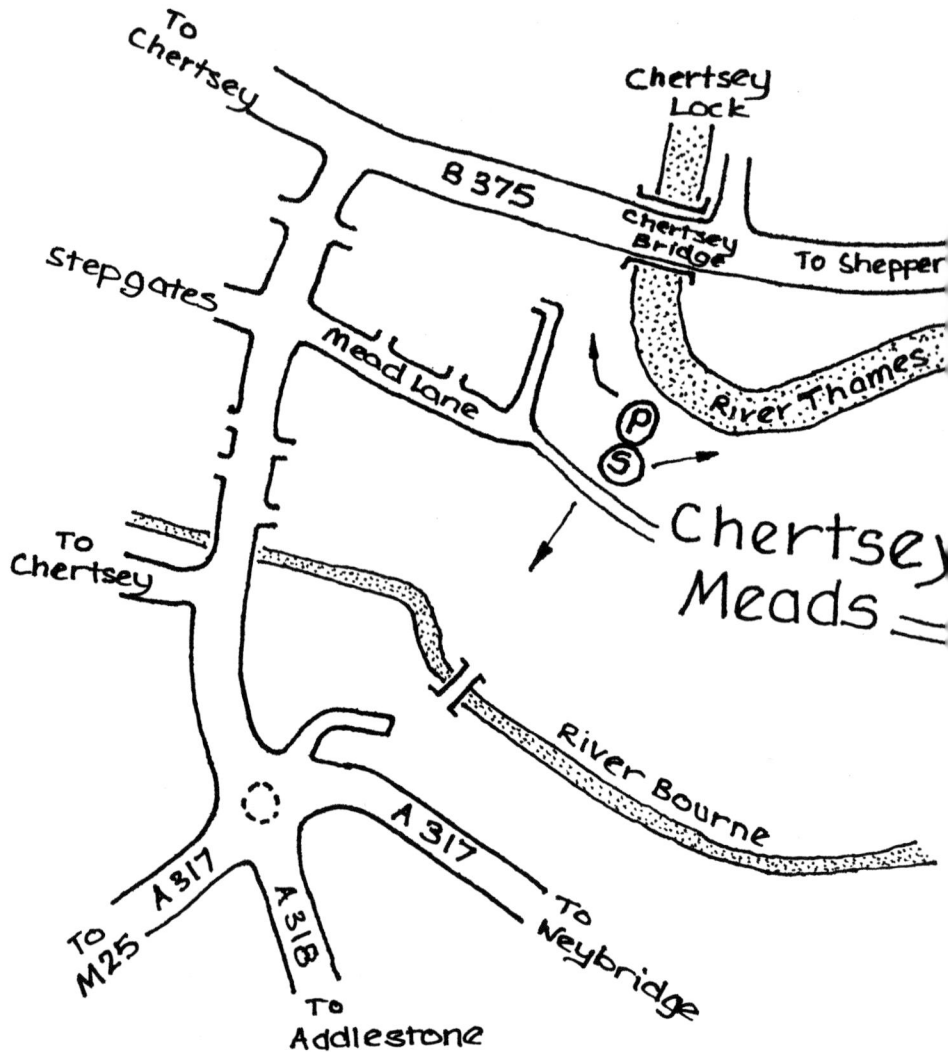

CHERTSEY MEADS have been cultivated as open fields since early medieval times; degenerate leeks still grow in the grass. It's a wide open place to enjoy fresh air and a sense of space.

PARKING : Designated car parks on the Meads, reached from Mead Lane off the Fordwater Road on the east side of Chertsey.

OPTIONS ; From the car park you can :-
(1) cross the grassland to walk on the banks of the River Thames, view Chertsey Bridge and simply watch the boats go by, or
(2) explore the paths around the Meads and follow the River Bourne.
Both options are detailed separately below.

The Chaffinch is a common bird that can be seen regularly, even hopping among the cars and the people in the car parks.

(1) TO THE THAMES

No problem as the car parks are adjacent.
It's pleasant enough to exercise dogs and
let children run but rather too public
for there to be much of wildlife value.
For those interested in natural history
it's better to cross over to The Bourne
as detailed below.

Over to the left (upstream)
the boatyards and moorings
add to the interest. There's
a way through to the main
road (B375), Chertsey Bridge
and Chertsey Lock.

29·8·1978

Shawtrey Bridge 1982

CHERTSEY BRIDGE

This has been a crossing point of great strategic importance since the Middle Ages. At first there was only a **ferry**; on February 21st 1300 Sibille the ferry woman and six men were paid three shillings for taking Edward I and his family across. Henry IV licensed a bridge - vital for rebels and defensive forces to skirt London.

The present bridge, designed by James Paine, was built 1780-5. This, and Staines Bridge, are the only two of architectural merit in the administrative county of Surrey. Paine lived in walking distance at Sayes Court (demolished) over the Meads at Addlestone, from 1772 when his practice went into decline. Domestic problems drove him to France where he died in 1789. Most of his notable work is in the Midlands and the North.

(2) TO THE BOURNE

NOT ALL THIS ROUTE IS MARKED ON THE MAP

Imagine the Meads comprise a rough rectangle with the start in the top left hand corner. This walk travels to bottom left and along to bottom right (the footbridge to Hamm Court) and back across the Meads to top left.

C. Howkins
17-5-1978

At the Chertsey end of the Meads a footpath
leads down across the field to the River
Bourne and a footbridge; don't cross the
river. Before this a cross-path heads off
over the Meads towards the bottom corner
over on your left. However, providing
ramblers do not invade crops, it is
usually tolerated for them to turn left at
the bridge and walk along the river bank
to the Hamm Court corner.

Walking between the two
bridges is further than
it looks ! Allow about
20 minutes straight
walking time.

Waterside plants embellish the
river's edge and the banks - the
white form of the comfrey, pale blue water forget-me-
nots, spikes of purple loosestrife and loose heads of
meadowsweet. Note also a weeping beech on the other
side. This tree was first raised in 1820.

Mallard, moorhens and kingfishers reward the quiet
walker if nobody has disturbed them previously. In
the winter, surface water on the Meads or in plough
furrows attract a wider range, including teal and
woodcock; even herons stalk the mud.

Similarly, quietness can be rewarded with close views
of water voles (illustrated with sketches made here in
1977). They feed on the vegetation, their blunt heads
showing they are not rats or "water rats".

The private lands over the river were once the famous
landscape garden of Woburn. This "ferme ornee" was
created by the noted landscape designer, William
Kent, for Philip Southcote, who bought the estate in
1735. Practically all sign of it has gone today.
Beyond the second footbridge (don't cross it) lies
Hamm Court (private), an early medieval moated site
 of which again little is
to be seen. This is
due in part to the
3rd Earl of Port-
more who vowed he
would leave to
his family nothing
of value for them to
inherit.

This end of the Meads verges up upon private properties. There is no exit as the Rivers Bourne and Thames almost meet.

You need to return to the car park. From the Hamm Court footbridge the footpath follows the Bourne back a little way before cutting over towards the Thames. Other paths are regularly used by walkers, following up the side of the ancient thorn hedges but every respect needs paying to the farmer's crops. Even grass is a crop. Short cuts can end in disaster in winter when surface water tends to collect!

A surfaced lane cuts across the centre of the Meads and when this is reached, turn left.

This fine open space is unusual in Surrey where most places have lost their open field system to later development. The Broadmead at Woking is another example as is the Burys down at Godalming.

CHOBHAM : Exploring a Medieval Village
Distance : 1 mile approx.

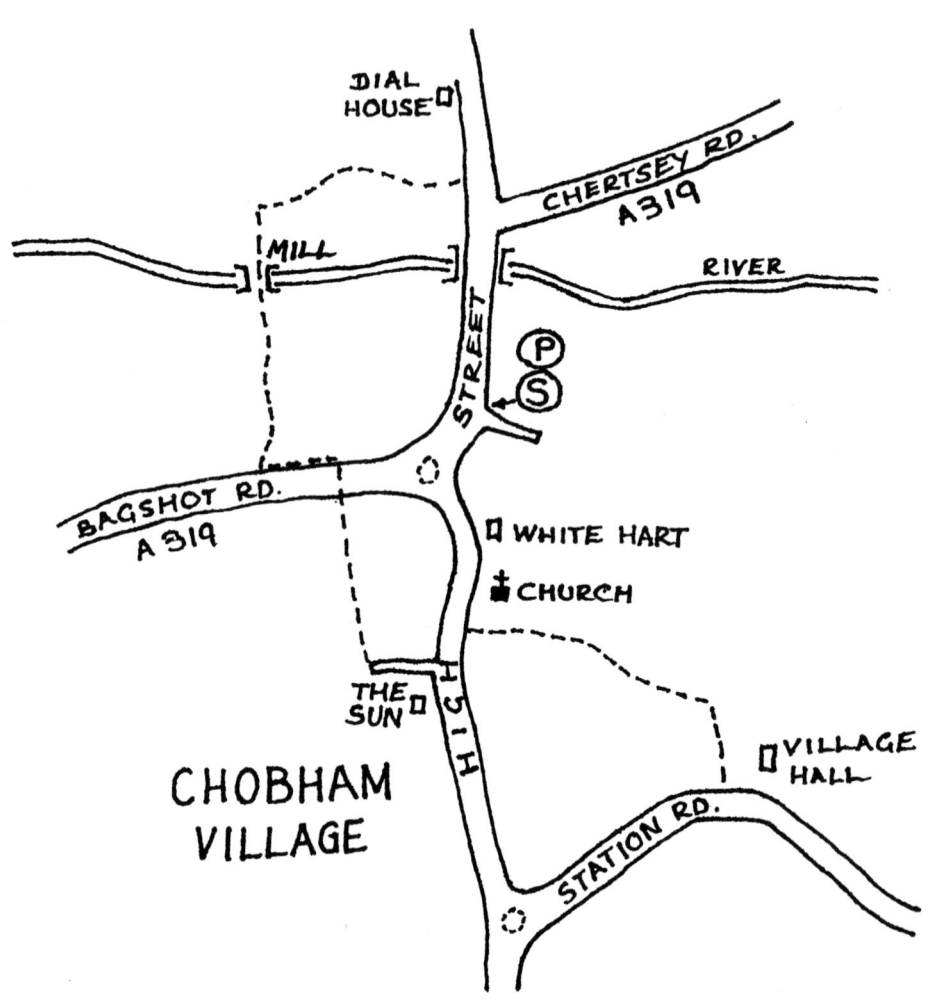

CHOBHAM was a farming settlement for Chertsey Abbey
still showing its medieval church and street pattern
today. Fine timber-framed buildings date from the break-
up of the Abbey estates in the 16th century following
the Dissolution of the Monasteries.

PARKING : Official car park off High Street.

BEGIN : From car park take the footpath out
to the cannon in the High Street.

THE CANNON is the second to stand here. The first was
given to Chobham by the War Office to commemorate Queen
Victoria's review of the troops on the nearby common in
1853. It had been a splendid military display, complete
with mock battles. Then in 1942 Chobham decided their
cannon had to go as scrap metal towards the war effort
but it was not forgotten. Enquiries in the 1970s
confirmed it had indeed been melted down but this present
one (of 1788) was located at the National Artillery
Museum and is on permanent loan. The villagers themselves rallied to produce locally a replica of its
carriage and the complete memorial was reinstated 1979.

COTTAGES : Behind the cannon stand
Cannon and Laurel Cottages, exposing to
view their 16th century timber framing.
Some half dozen such period pieces stand
in the village centre.

CROSS OVER THE ROAD - FOLLOW the
footpath along to the RIGHT.

It's an attractive path under the trees along the banks
of a stream (golden with daffodils in Spring). The
waterway was the overflow leat from Town Mill. After
the mill was demolished in 1967 the leat often ran dry
until villagers tapped water from the nearby R. Bourne.

NOTE : the iron-gated entrance to Chobham House
opposite Chertsey Road for later in this walk.

COTTAGES. Opposite, on the corner of Chertsey Road
stands another fine 16th century timber-framed group,
The Homestead and Aden Cottage. Ahead, on the left,
stands Dial House of 1720, one of the notable 18th
century homes in the centre. Its front elevation has
a large sundial designed to function at an angle as
the house doesn't face due south. Turn back.

RETURN to Chobham House.
FOLLOW the drive till the footpath skirts off
to the right.
                    The path sneaks round the grounds of
The Grange (destroyed) with many fine trees. The
very rugged silvery grey bark of the False Acacia
is particularly eyecatching.
                    The Bourne is reached
where it cascades through the remains of the sluices
of the former Town Mill, dating from c.1780. The
milling ceased in 1960. All the trees through here
are popular with a wide variety of bird life.

Chobham

17

JOIN THE DRIVEWAY
CONTINUE AHEAD TO THE
   BAGSHOT ROAD
CROSS IT AND TURN LEFT
AT SCHOOL SIGN TURN
   RIGHT INTO FOOTPATH

Here you escape the bustle of
the High Street and get peeps
over the wall to the backs of
the buildings. They include 16th,
18th and 19th century work together
with some fine modern work built to match its neighbours

TURN LEFT at the end, to emerge into the
HIGH STREET, but....

                        by turning right there's a detou
to the old shrubby cemetery, rich with wildlife and
with a grassy path round it. Specimen trees have been
planted between this and the new cemetery and a path
continues the line of the drive out to Penny Pot Lane.
There you can turn right to Bagshot Road and right again
to return to the cannon - narrow and busy at times-
an extra mile on the walk. The path crosses the former
grounds of Hilling's Rose Nursery, best known for the
pink scented shrub rose "Marguerite Hilling".

AT THE HIGH STREET CROSS OVER TO THE CHURCH

CHURCH - The church of St. Lawrence is a beautiful
building dating from c.1080, with the original little
Norman windows showing in part over the slightly later
arches in the nave. These nave arcades were built just
as taste changed from the Norman style to that known as
"Early English" and the transition shows.
      The greatest treasure is the 16th century wooden
font, installed contrary to church law. Only four can
be found in the country and two of them are in Surrey:
this one and another at Ash.
      The item with the most interesting story is the
plain blue marble slab set in the nave floor in front
of the chancel step. Here, in the reign of Elizabeth I,

they buried a former
Archbishop of York,
Nicholas Heath, who
had also been Lord
Chancellor. He refused to
take the 2nd Act of Supremacy
oath, making Elizabeth Head
of the Church of England, for
which he was deprived of office
and put in the Tower of London.
Eventually he was allowed to
retire to Chobham Park and there
he was visited by Her Majesty.

nave
arcade
c.1170

**Leave church and turn into
the SOUTHERN CHURCHYARD.**

The wooden west porch is medieval.
The tower, built of broken sarsens from the common at
West End, as was Chertsey Abbey, dates from c.1400.
It's the finest medieval stone tower in N.W.Surrey.
The lead spire is also rare in Surrey (see Thames
Ditton and Godalming). The south wall shows another
material scavenged from the fields being richly used.

The churchyard blue cedar was given by the famous local
nurseryman, Anthony Waterer, and planted by Lady Walpole
in 1902 to commemorate the coronation of Edward VII.

LEAVE churchyard by iron gate in S.E. corner.

Looking left along the top of the cricket green, the
large specimen tree is an English walnut, for which Surrey
was once the premier county. They're thinly scattered
today.

FOLLOW the path round the green to the HALL.

The Village Hall was built of local bricks in 1888,
restored 1989. It shows the Victorian sense of
community and social provision at a time when the locals
were getting enough free time to use such a hall.

TURN RIGHT out of the Village
Hall car park and follow the
cottages along to the
mini-roundabout.

First, look left and see
the little square classical
building (Antiques shop).
It was built as Chobham's
first Electric Sub-station!
It's now preserved.

TURN RIGHT at the
mini-roundabout.

WALK the length of
the HIGH STREET back
to the cannon and the
car park.

There's attractive townscaping
all along here, enhanced by the
fall of the land and the curve of
the street. "The Sun" is likely to
catch the eye first and that dates
from the 18th century while the "White
Hart" following dates from the 16th
and 17th centuries.

COBHAM – The semaphore Tower on Chatley Heath
before restoration.
SEE NEXT WALK

21

COBHAM : Heath and Semaphore Tower

Distance : Wander at Will

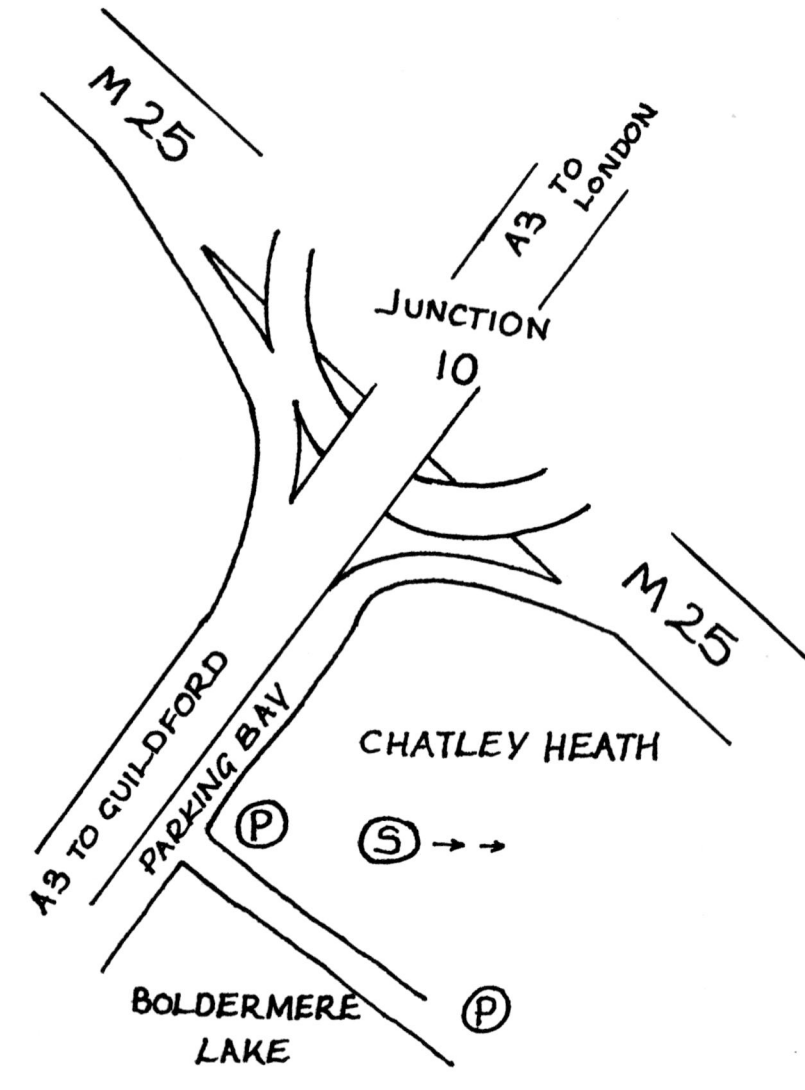

LOCATION AND PARKING : Beside Boldermere Pond
                      east side of the A3.

A3 NORTHBOUND TRAFFIC drive past the site and
   take the slip-road for the M25. Go round
   the roundabout sandwiched between the A3
   and the M25 and leave by the exit for the
   A3 Southbound (Guildford and Portsmouth).
   A lay-by for parking is immediately on
   the left but go halfway along it and turn
   left, signposted Car Parks and Semaphore.

A3 SOUTHBOUND TRAFFIC take the slip-road for
   the M25 but cross the roundabout as though
   to merge with the A3 again but before that
   you'll pass the parking bay listed above
   and turn left as per northbound traffic.

BACK LANES from Effingham - see road map or
   Ordnance Survey map to save getting lost.

BEGIN : Having turned off the A3 there's a
   choice of two car parks. The second is
   the quieter but the first has the
   refreshment kiosk at which you can buy the
   guide book to the tower and a map leaflet
   describing the heathland location. In
   this car park is also displayed a map of
   the commons, clearly showing the route to
   the tower.

SEMAPHORE TOWER OPENING TIMES

   April to September: Sat. and Sun. afternoons
        and Wednesday afternoons in school
        holidays plus Bank Holiday afternoons.

   Obviously opening times may change during
   the life of this book but they can be
   checked with the Tower Manager on Cobham
   62762.

THE WALK TO THE TOWER is by following the main
track out of the car park, away from the A3. Keep
going uphill and you'll get there ! Allow about
twenty minutes. The path is deep sand in places
which might not please anyone in open-toed sandals !
It's also difficult for pushchairs and wheelchairs.
It's a beautiful walk through woodlands and over
heathlands.

THE SEMAPHORE TOWER is the latest of West Surrey's
heritage centres. It was restored and opened to the
public in 1989 as a joint venture between the Surrey
Historic Buildings Trust and Surrey County Council,
to mark the Council's centenary.

The illustration was sketched in 1981 when the tower
was derelict but before it was burnt out inside (1984).
Visitors will now appreciate how carefully it has
been cleaned and restored, including the provision of
a signalling system which is demonstrated to visitors.

The story of the Tower is told more than adequately
by the displays inside but basically, it was built
in 1822 as part of an improved signalling system
between the Admiralty in London and Portsmouth
Naval Dockyard. Instead of the shutter system tried
previously, this tower sent messages by raising and
lowering a semaphore arm, like old-fashioned railway
signals. Invented in 1812, the system only lasted
until the invention of the electric telegraph in 1847,
when all the towers including this one were closed.
There were fifteen towers and stations along the route,
passing their messages at the rate of about six words
per minute; this is the only surviving restored example.
It would also have been the most important as from here
another line to Plymouth was started but abandoned
after building only nine of the stations.

THERE IS AN ADMISSION CHARGE
In 1989 it was £1 for adults; 50p for children
          and old age pensioners.

BIRDLIFE

The crossbill (right),
siskin (bottom) and the redpoll
(overleaf) are three of the birds
attracted to this area now that the
birch and pine are plentiful and
mature enough to fruit. All three are
seed-eaters, with the crossbill having a
bill specialised for opening pine cones to get at the
protein-rich seeds. The regeneration of such trees
over so much of the southern heathlands is attracting
these birds in increasing numbers and the abundance of
food is encouraging them to stay longer; so much so
that their status as winter migrants is changing very
gradually as some stay south to breed. When so many
heaths are dry, Boldermere lake is an added attraction
here as seed-eaters must have water to compensate for
their dry diet.

PINE AND BIRCH

Enough is enough and measures are
now being taken to restrict the further development
of pinewoods. They're invading the open heathlands
and those are a much more precious habitat. They're
only found on the Atlantic fringe of N.W.Europe but
even there are subject to great variation. For example,
the birch can be terribly
invasive in England
but is not so
in Denmark.

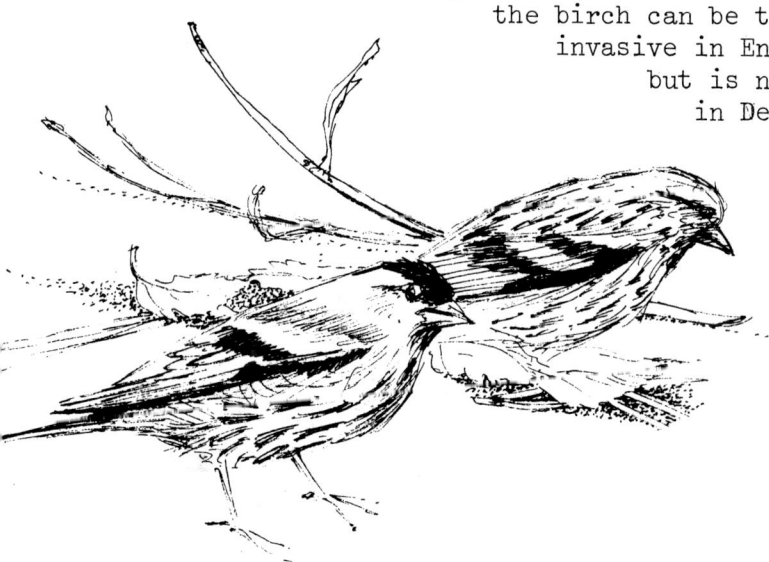

Thus these places are of
international importance.
Visitors are often
invited to help in
the conservation
here by pulling up
pine seedlings on
their walks. Look
for a notice on the
board in the car park.

TOADSTOOLS

In late
summer and early autumn
you can regularly find, under
the birch trees, those red toadstools
with white spots that appear in fairy tale
book illustrations. These "fly agarics" are
well known for being poisonous but this is not
so throughout the whole of their range in the
Northern Hemisphere. If you have eaten them
abroad or have them in a foreign cookery book do
not be tempted to try British ones. One of the
poisons is a constituent of rocket fuel but it
certainly won't make you feel on top of the world !

BROOMS AND BRICKS

The heathlands need us to
conserve them today since
the old management practices
have died out. No longer are
the tree seedlings destroyed by
the grazing of sheep and cattle.
No longer is the tall ling heather
cut for making brooms, as indeed
was the birch. No longer is the
mature gorse harvested for fuel.
Gorse burns slowly with great heat
and so faggots of the stems were
highly prized for firing brick
kilns, especially in Surrey
during the Victorian building
boom.

BOLDERMERE - the pond by the car parks.

TAKE CARE not to let children and dogs run heedless across the road between the pond and the car parks.

PUSHCHAIRS AND WHEELCHAIRS are provided with a surface path to the waterside beginning on the road at a point between the two car parks.

BIRDS AND FLOWERS still flourish here although they have declined since the pond has become so popular for recreation. Windsurfers don't even leave a peaceful space in the centre for the birds. Nevertheless there are still many more flowers here than out on the common and several birds nest successfully, including coots, moorhens, mallard and Canada geese.

Come early in the morning after a stormy night, especially in the winter, and see which wildfowl have sought out shelter. Of the less common species in this area, pochard, wigeon, gadwall and shoveler have all been recorded. For more detailed information on this site see "Enjoying Wisley's Birds" by David and June Elliott and Chris Howkins.

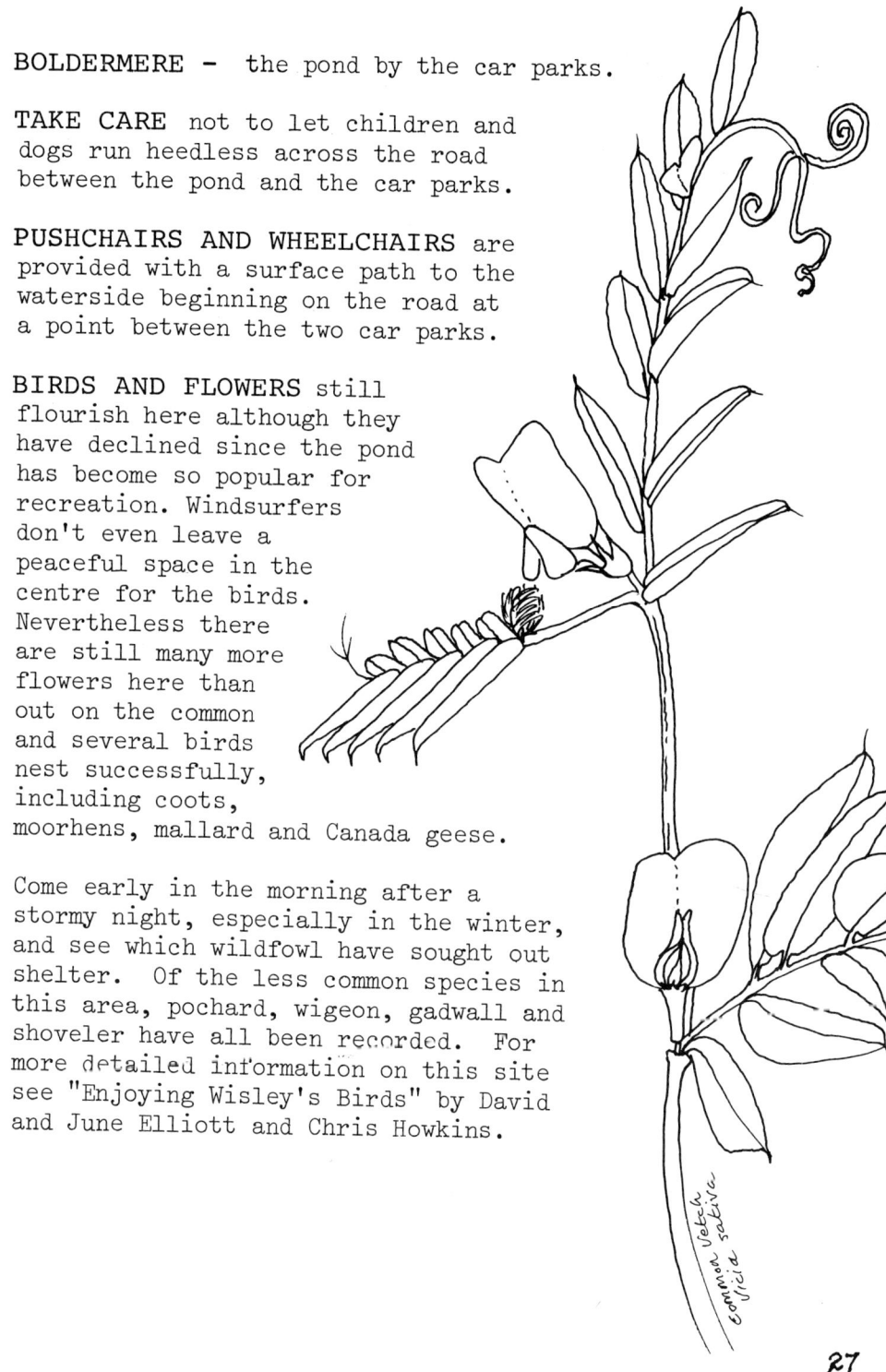

Common Vetch
Vicia sativa

27

LALEHAM : Historic Thames-side Village

Distance: 1 mile

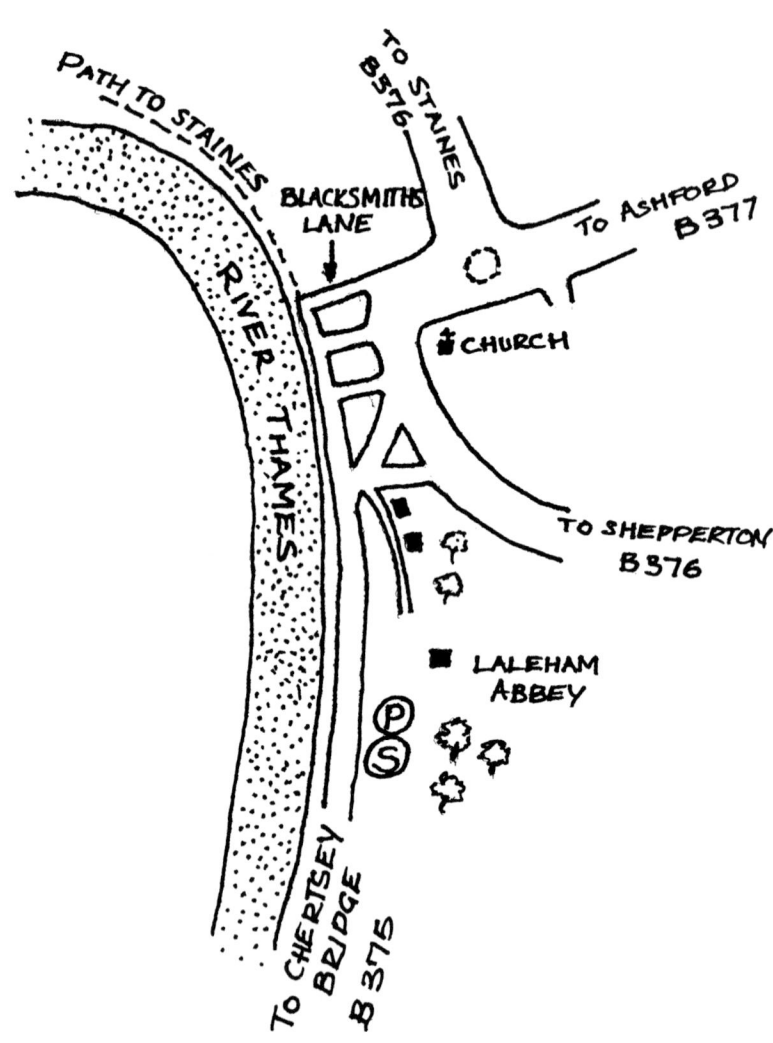

PARKING : Car parks are provided beside the riverfront approached from Chertsey Bridge (off B375) or from the centre of Laleham, signposted to the river.
Avoid peak leisure periods.

LALEHAM, Middlesex, administered by Surrey County Council, is one of several attractive Thames-side villages, with brick houses, walled gardens and narrow side ways that go down to the river.

No longer is this a centre for commercial river traffic. Instead, the waterfront is given over to residential and recreational use, attracting many people at peak leisure times - to feed the ducks, saunter across the grass in the sunshine and to watch the river and the boats go by. Very nice it is too but there is much more to Laleham than that but only a little of its long history can be highlighted here......

BEGIN : The Car Parks on the riverfront are on the edge of a grange or farm administered by Westminster Abbey, back in the Middle Ages. The lands bordered those of nearby Chertsey Abbey, occasioning some unholy disputes which had to be settled in court.
The farm was followed by a succession of houses until the Government did a deal with the 2nd Earl of Lucan who then became the owner. He brought in the Prince Regent's architect, John Buonarotti Papworth who built the present house, to an advanced design for the early years of last century. It stands through the trees behind the car parks.

THE WALK through the trees here is so rewarding because there are so many different species which include hornbeams, now far less common than formerly when they were grown in coppices to provide firewood.

PATHS towards the village lead out onto recreation fields and plenty of scope to wander and enjoy the trees. These lands were snatched back from developers in 1931 when they'd only built three of the 300 houses proposed. £300 was spent on trees instead.

HEADING TOWARDS THE VILLAGE the paths lead onto the driveway and so to a thatched cottage, attributed to Papworth, in the "cottage ornee" style

Next of interest is The Coverts; a refined brick house of Georgian simplicity. It's an early example dating from about 1700. Notice that its window frames are flush with the walls - a design later outlawed as a fire risk.

TURN RIGHT out of the cul-de-sac and the large house on the bend ahead is Muncaster House. It's always been Laleham's claim that the oldest parts were purchased in 1819 by the Rev. John Buckland and his brother-in-law, the Rev. Thomas Arnold and that here Buckland started the country's first Prep. School. This claim has recently been questioned.

Arnold worked with the older children to prepare them for University until he himself moved on to become the famous headmaster of Rugby School. Both families are buried in Laleham churchyard.

Elder in bud.

CONTINUE along the side street.
TURN LEFT at the main road.

The old village centre is an attractive knot although
busy with traffic at peak periods. Following round
to the left you'll find the old parish church with
its ruby brickwork harmonising with the houses.
Unfortunately its Norman interior is usually denied
to visitors as the church has to be kept locked.
Outside you can find the Arnold graves, see the
early brick Lucan chapel with its diapering and the
distinctive tower dated 1732. The tower has broad
rustications in brick to echo the stone ones on
the house opposite, all trying to make an earlier
Laleham look fashionable.

TURN LEFT DOWN BLACKSMITH'S LANE opposite the
church and next to the above mentioned house.

This is an attractive route down to the river, with
a range of architecture, smartly maintained, and with
the prospect of colour and interest in the little
front gardens.

ON THE RIVERFRONT there's a 2¼ mile walk to
Staines (turn right) but turn left to return
along the riverbank to the car parks.

On your left the boundary is supported by posts
bearing the arms of the City of London. They are
one of several different reminders along this stretch
of the Thames that it was once within the juristiction
of the City and Corporation.

Emerging out onto the grassland
you're liable to find flocks of
mallard and Canada geese seeking
food off the visitors. Coot and
moorhen also appear and there
were tufted duck on the day this
page was prepared. Numbers drop
in spring when they go off to
breed.

OTTERSHAW : Woodlands
Distance : wander at will

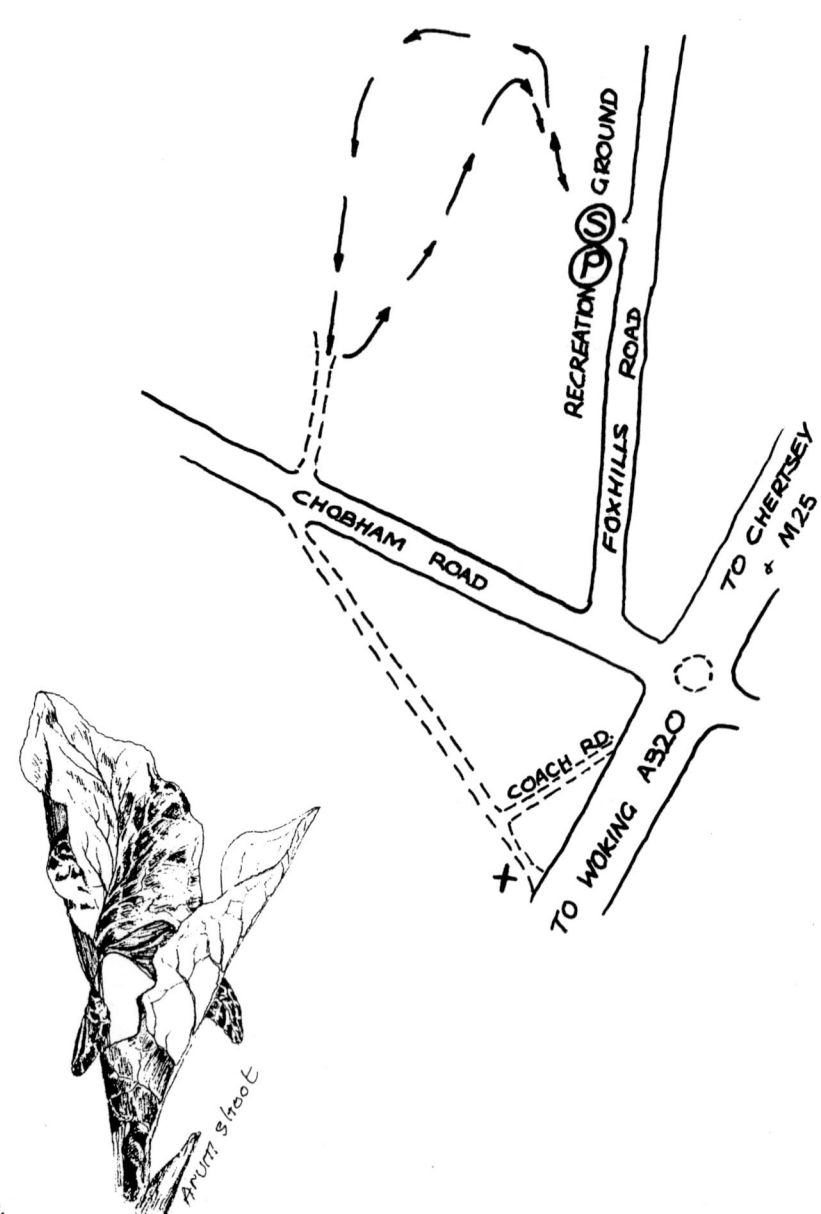

CAR PARKING -

Off FOXHILLS ROAD;
there is an entrance
on the left through
the hedge into a
small parking area.
Sometimes it over-
flows into roadside
parking.

BEGIN - There is no prescribed walk here.
Wander at will and enjoy being able
to do just that.

The site is the recreation ground but don't imagine a
flat playing field with a surrounding chain link fence
and a howling wind slicing across it.

Here a long narrow field slides out from under the
trees of a wooded knoll, with hedges or trees all
around. Families can picnic or play on the grass
or watch the local sports teams; there is an area
protected for children's play and toilet facilities.
There's also the chance to wander off and explore
the more natural areas including a walk up over the
knoll into the woodlands.

The map shows that by taking the woodland ride at the
back of the knoll it is possible to walk down onto the
Chobham Road and back round to the car park or even to
extend that further and walk up to the next hilltop
with the church on it, and so back to the car. The
main road is not very pleasant here to walk beside.

Earlier this century the knoll was covered with gorse and heather but that heathland has now been overcome by regenerating woodland. Just a few straggly ling plants survived in 1989, doomed to die in the next season or so.

Hundreds of birch trees shade out the light and make dense thickets on one side. Among the birches scrubby oaks push through and will one day win. This sort of scrubby woodland is invading a large proportion of Surrey's open countryside and so measures are being taken in some places to try and reduce it. The habitats that it destroys are more valuable and the new habitat it creates is not so popular with wildlife as might be imagined. Here, nevertheless, there is much to enjoy, from the mosses and toadstools, to wild flowers and of course the trees.

Up on the top there is a fine stand of mature Scots Pines which have suppressed all other growth to leave a soft carpet of needles between the trunks to wander over.

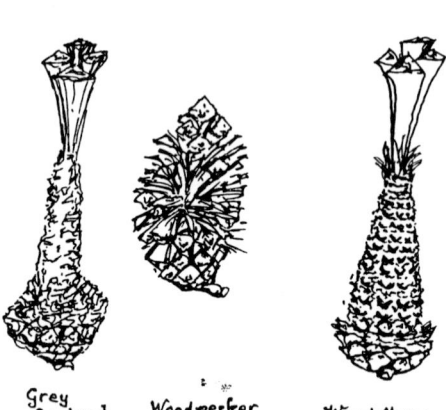

Grey Squirrel   Woodpecker   Wood Mouse

By studying the fallen cones it is possible to decide which species have been attacking them to reach their nutritious seeds.

Beyond the pines some beech saplings have been planted and are growing fast. Soon these too will shade out all other growth and there will be more open woodland floor to walk over. This will be very different – soft with leaf mould instead of needle peat. The difference will show particularly well in autumn when each sports its own range of toadstools. Little red ones with white undersides are Russula mairei under beech but Russula emetica under pine; both look identical.

It's the oak trees that are
intriguing up on the knoll.
Some are small and twisted,
contorting themselves into such
curious shapes that it is difficult
to imagine that the same species is one
of our most important forest trees for
hardwood timber. The difference is not
due entirely to the stunting effects of
the shallow dry soil, deficient in nutrients.
Genetics play their part too. Acorns from
these trees will grow like this in conditions
thought far more favourable because they have
inherited such characteristics.

Formerly the twisted
scrub oaks were valued for providing strong but shaped
timber for particular jobs. Nowadays nursery stock drawn
upon by the conservationists when replanting oak, is
derived from EEC approved acorns and they of course
were collected from the finest timber
trees - tall and straight.

With these native oaks
(Quercus robur) there's also
a few Turkey Oaks (Quercus
cerris). The lobes of its
leaves are pointed.
    It was introduced
into Britain about 1735
and comes from S.E.Europe
and Turkey.

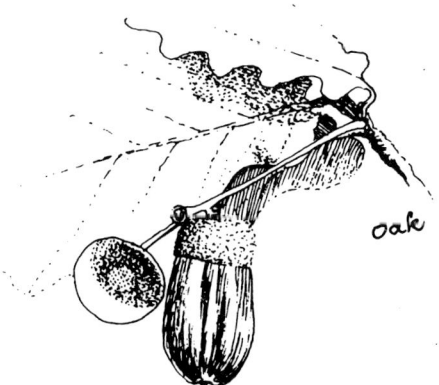

oak

RIPLEY: Grassland, Woodland and Waterside
Distance: 3 miles approx.

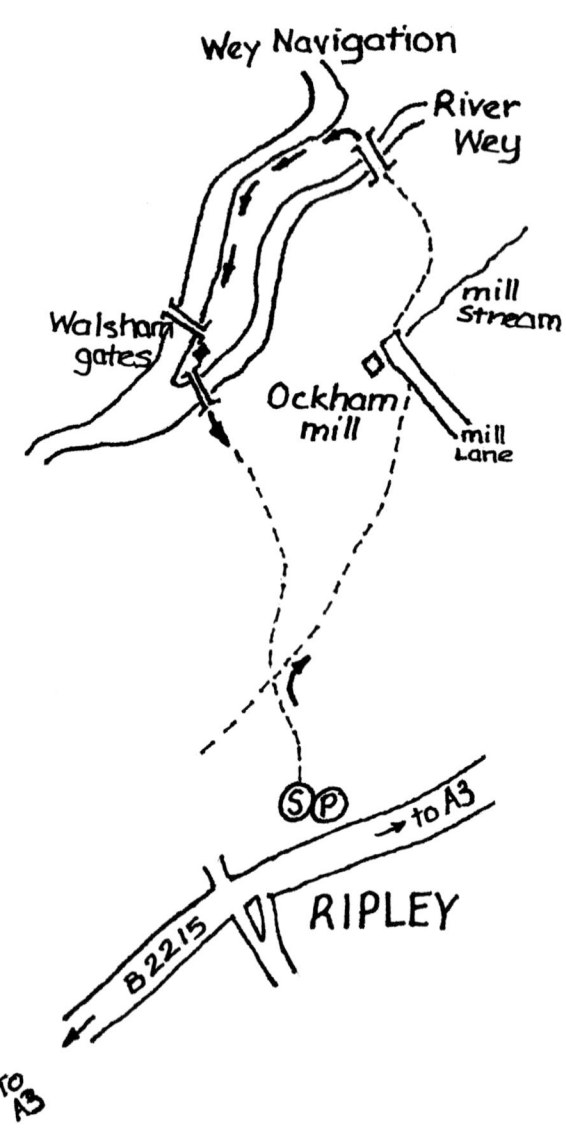

CAR PARKING : Beside the village green of
Ripley, on the left of the
street (B2215) if travelling
towards London. The street is
the old A3 and links at both ends
with the new A3.

BEGIN : From the car park follow the gravel
track out over the village green and
keep to this main track, round to the
right, heading for the woods at the
top of the green

During a good summer the long grass here-
abouts becomes rich with butterflies.
Grasshoppers can be heard chirruping
away on a warm day too and that's
not a sound so easy to enjoy in
Surrey today.
The shorter grass gets
a regular stabbing over by platoons
of starlings. How they synchronise
their flock movements is still a
mystery – something to wonder at without
the enjoyment being stifled with scientific explanation.
Starlings only became such common birds in Surrey by the
end of the 19th century. Before then they were a shy
bird of wooded country, nesting in tree holes, and back
before that they were only to be found on the sea cliffs.
Other sea birds developing inland lifestyles are the
gulls and can be seen on this green in the winter months;
usually the black-headed (with a black spot behind their
eye) but look out for other species too.
The little black
and white birds darting over the short grass for insects
or swooping up to snatch them from the low air are the
pied wagtails.

Starlings.

Continue into the woods and follow the path round to the stream and across the bridge. Continue until you reach Mill Lane. This path can be wet in winter.

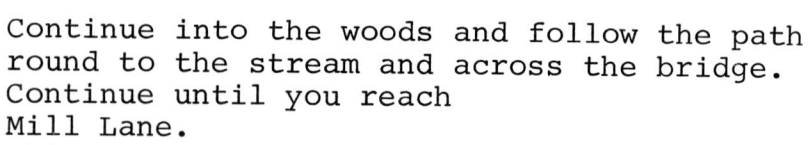

Woods come in different types according to the species of tree and the habitat they create. If you explore over to the right the green runs into a wood of small close oaks with an undercarpet of sheep's fescue grass — very different from the wood the path has been running through with its ground flora of brambles, holly and ivy; all indicating that the wood is not of a great age. By the bridge the mature boundary oaks with their ancient hedge banks record far older landscapes. The ground flora here includes wood anemones and moschatel to confirm that this has been wooded for many generations.

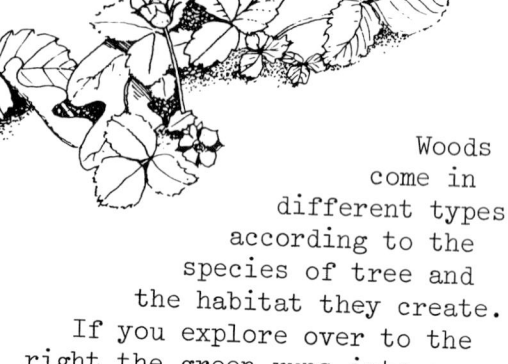

Old woods support the greatest range of wildlife. Willow Warbler illustrated.

At Mill Lane turn left.
Follow the road to Ockham Mill and round to
the right after crossing the mill stream.

Millwater House was home to the landscape artist
F. W. Hulme (1816-1844) who exhibited local scenes
at the Royal Academy. The house was later enlarged
by Sir Frederick Stokes (1860-1927), the civil
engineer and inventor, who designed the sluices and
gates for the Aswan Dam (1901).

Ockham Mill Cottage was used as a retreat from London
bombing during World War II by Surrey's most famous
architect, Sir Edwin Lutyens.

Ockham Mill, with its associated houses and farm,
makes a very attractive hamlet, especially with the
mill stream still gushing under the road into a
pool before flowing off to join the River Wey.
A mill has stood here since at least the 13th century
although the present mill
dates from 1862 - a fine
example of industrial
architecture of its time.

Through by Ockham Mill

FOLLOW THE TRACK
round to the right
and keep to it as
it crosses the fields
to the footbridge
over the River Wey
and so up to the
towpath of the Wey
Navigation.

This route is "Wharf
Lane" from when corn came
this way from canal barges
at the wharf on the Wey
Navigation - and flour made
the return journey. From the
footbridge you can peer down
into the river and see the
footings of the old bridge that
carried the wagons across. The wharf and its associated
buildings have all gone. Only the nettles and elder
bushes indicate former human activity.

TURN LEFT.
Follow the towpath to Walsham Gates.

The canal opened in 1653, making it one of the first
long-distance schemes in the country. Walsham is one
the most beautiful and historic spots on the whole
route of 19½ miles. The lock is the last survivor
of the early design, being square instead of oblong;
early craft were broad not narrow. It's also the
last one to retain its grassy sides.

The little bridge is 18th century (don't cross it
if you wish to stay on this route ¡) and still has the
shallow steps for horses. The lock cottage, recently
restored, has Wedgwood chimney pots. Beside it, the
"paddles" in the lock gates are also a rare survival,
showing the early system whereby they were lifted by
hand and held in place with the attached pin.

FOLLOW the path
past the cottage
and round to the
left to cross
the weir.

Guelder Rose fruits.

Here the River
Wey and the Wey
Navigation part
company.
      The river
foams over the weir to go
off to Weybridge via Wisley
and Byfleet,while the canal
goes off to Weybridge via New
Haw and Addlestone.
            The pool was altered in the 1930s
to improve the flow and so reduce flooding. Before
that the lock-keeper could be called upon to row the
schoolchildren from the Pyrford side across the flood
waters to go to school in Ripley. Nowadays Pyrford
has its own schools. Floods are rare but even so,
after winter rains this can be an exciting place of
rushing waters. Look out for grey wagtails (illustrated).

Cross the weir and follow the
path back to Ripley Green.

STAINES : Historic Town Ramble

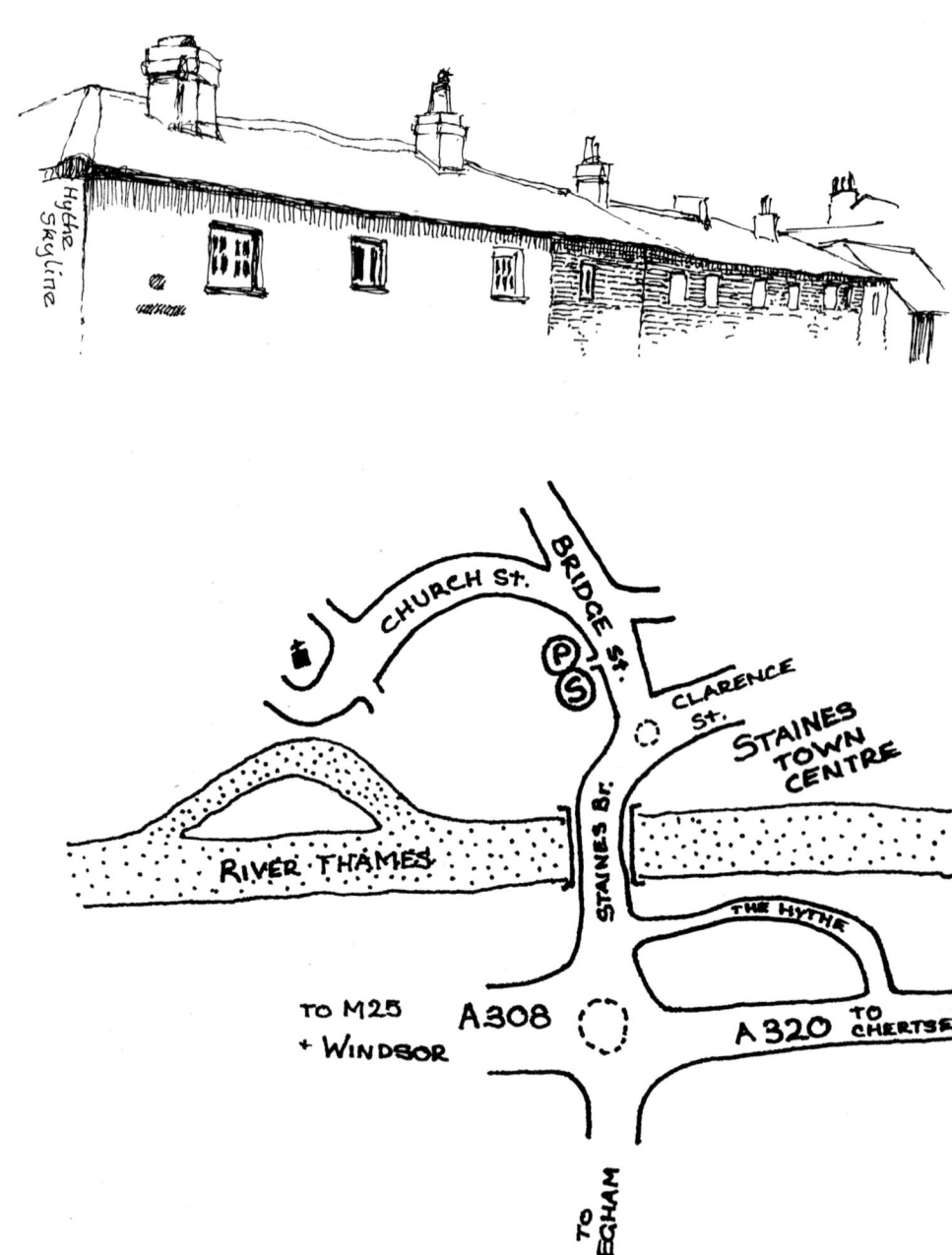

Hythe Skyline

CHURCH St.

BRIDGE St.

CLARENCE St.

STAINES TOWN CENTRE

RIVER THAMES

STAINES BR.

THE HYTHE

TO M25 + WINDSOR

A308

A320 TO CHERTSE

TO EGHAM

PARKING : Car park off Bridge Street.

Limited parking in Egham Hythe
but not when the pubs are busy.
Town Centre car parks not far off.
Limited car parking in Church Street.

THE ROUTE : This route has been planned as
a loop so that it can be halved
if wished; first, over Staines
Bridge to the Hythe and second,
along to the parish church.

Since Roman times Staines has been an important bridge
point on the Thames. Stage coaches came this way in
their thousands to reach the West Country and in Egham
south of the river can still be seen one of the inns,
a milestone and the pump for laying the dust.

TO THE HYTHE

**TURN RIGHT out of the Bridge Street car park
and walk to the bridge.**

You climb slightly uphill, out of the old town ditch
site for this was the undeveloped side of early Staines,
the side vulnerable to flooding. The old centre was
on the higher gravel beds where today's town centre
still stands.

The foundation stone for the present Staines Bridge
was laid by the Duke of Clarence in 1829. He
returned as King George IV in 1832 for the official
opening. It was not altered until widened in 1958.
The architect was not, as has been claimed, the
John Rennie of Waterloo Bridge fame, for he had died
in 1821. It's the work of his sons, George and John.
This, and Chertsey Bridge, are the only two bridges
of architectural merit in the administrative County
of Surrey.

Until the creation of the Thames Conservancy in 1857 the river was administered by the Mayors, later Lord Mayors, of London. This was the final stretch of their juristiction, marked on the bank by the London Stone (see below).

Over to the left, on the south bank, is the site of the prehistoric settlement, and, by the roundabout at the end of the bridge, the factory site where Lagonda cars were made. The first Lagonda was built in Staines in 1906 and the company continued here until 1947 when the site was badly flooded.
      Another famous engineering company, Petters, then took over until the 1986 merger with the Lister Company of Bristol.

CROSS THE BRIDGE and CHANGE to the DOWNSTREAM SIDE.

LOOKING OVER THE BRIDGE - DOWNSTREAM SIDE -
you view The Hythe, the old name for a waterfront or harbour. Here, when the river was a main highway, the boats pulled in. From here the earlier bridges arched across to Staines on the former Middlesex shore. You look down on an attractive congestion of brick and tile, approached along the line of a fine old terrace of cottages. To reach it...

TURN LEFT OFF THE BRIDGE

Immediately as you turn there's a white post in the grass. Bearing the heraldic arms of the City of London, it's a former taxation marker. Hundreds were set up at each entry point into the juristiction of the Corporation of London following the 1861 Coal and Wine Duties Continuance Act. All coal passing here was taxed to raise funds for the public benefit of London. Such charges were abolished in 1890 but they had enabled the abolition of tolls on Staines Bridge back in 1871 - cause for local celebration.

COURAGE

COURAGE

Egham Hythe
after rain.

IN THE HYTHE

You'll find it delightfully congested between the old
buildings, giving the right 'feel' for a waterfront.
Many of the buildings are older than they look. Even
those of 18th century Georgian red brick may disguise
an older heart. Such is the case with the Jolly Farmer
(illustrated) which goes back to the 17th century.
With so little room here the sites were continually being
modernised or rebuilt upon.

Hythe End House was the home
of William Carpenter, a coach builder in the last
century but not just any old coach builder. This one
had members of the royal family as patrons !

RETURN TO THE CAR PARK

TO CHURCH STREET - LEFT OUT OF THE CAR PARK
AND FOLLOW THE ROAD ROUND.

Looking ahead across the road junction there is a yellow
brick house of 1820 which has seen some changes. First
it was part of a mustard mill on the site but that was
cleared away to make room for a railway line to West
Drayton. The house became the station, known as Staines
West. The last train ran in 1981 and now everything
has been cleared away again, leaving only the house.

Church Street curves through enough surviving 18th century
houses to give a dignified Georgian 'feel' to this
quarter. Here came the Quakers, meeting in Stainton
House, behind which is their burial ground. They were
an enterprising group which, in the London area, became
noted for brewing. Staines was no exception and the
greatest of its Quaker families, the Ashbys, began brewing
here, at no.57 at the end of the road. The brewhouse
survives (best seen from round the corner). Then they
expanded the site over the road, later sold out to
H.and G. Simmonds and now part of the Courage company.
When the site was remodelled in the 1970s the old
brewery tower was incorporated into the modern.

THE
BELLS

COURAGE

CHURCH STREET

47

LOWER END OF CHURCH STREET

The road curves down towards the river where, in the
Edwardian summers they held children's regattas. The
18th century character is enhanced by The Bells, which
used to be just The Bell. Perhaps it took its name from
the church bell that tolled from opposite.

The church is set back in a rather wild churchyard,
screened by trees and unexpectedly rural. The tower
bears a plaque recording the long-held belief that it's
the work of Inigo Jones. That idea has been squashed.

The association with Inigo Jones might have arisen
from his being Surveyor to the King and it was the
king, James I, who was Lord of the Manor.

Inside, the stained glass records the signing of the
Magna Carta at nearby Runnymede. Three other windows
were given by Kaiser Wilhelm to commemorate Augusta
Byng, the Staines girl who became his children's
nanny.

Round behind the churchyard the former Lammas lands,
used for common cultivation by the local people, have
been preserved as a recreation ground. There, within
the railings of the children's area, is a replica of
the 13th century London Stone referred to above.

RETURN TO THE CAR PARK

**There's more of interest to find around
Staines despite all the modern developments.**

Staines has been a trading centre for centuries.
The earliest recorded charter dates from 1218 but as
that's for changing the market day to Friday from
Sunday, to please the Church, it's obviously not the
first. The Friday market continued until the middle
of last century and a plaque on the traffic island by
Debenhams records the site. Originally the market may
well have been held in Church Street.

Staines 1987

49

STONEHILL : Heathland, Woods and Ponds

Distance : Wander at will

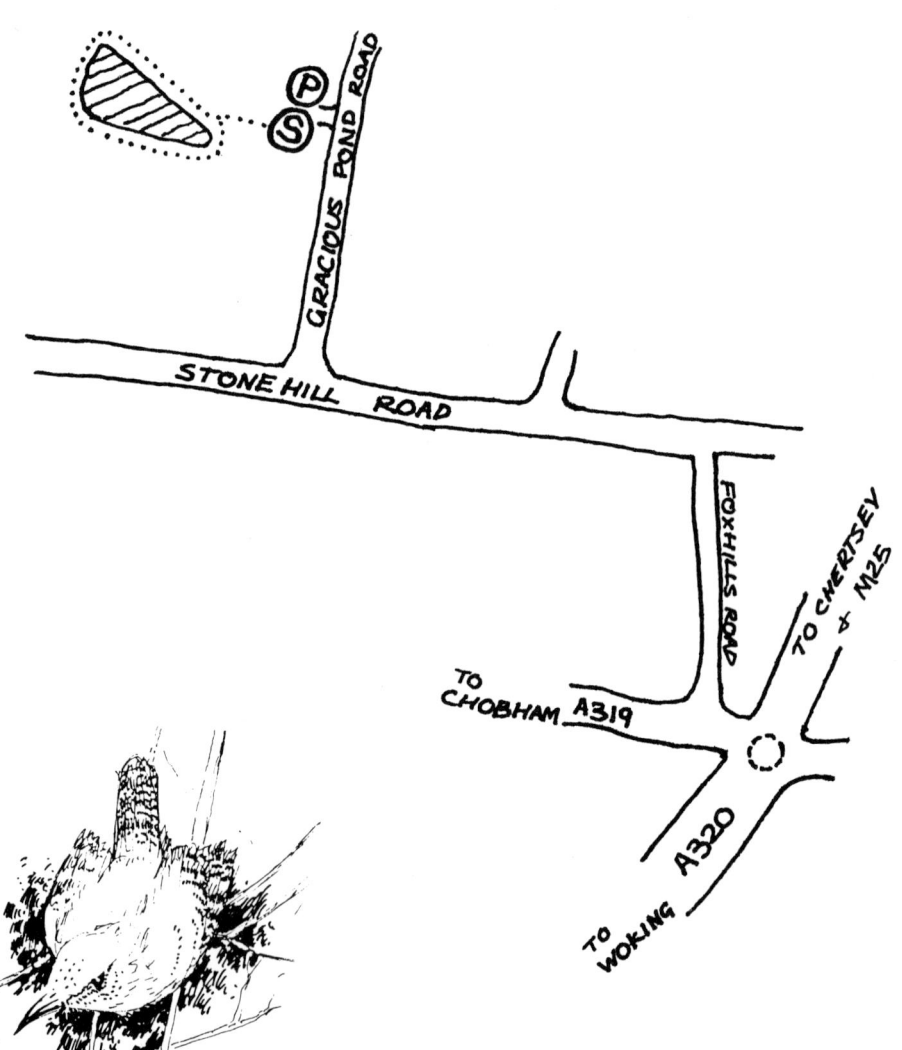

GRACIOUS POND ROAD

STONE HILL ROAD

FOXHILLS ROAD

TO CHOBHAM A319

TO CHERTSEY & M25

TO WOKING A320

CAR PARK : OFF GRACIOUS POND ROAD.
There's a designated parking area
on the edge of the heath, on the
left if you've come up from the
Stonehill Road.

BEGIN : NO PRESCRIBED ROUTE.
Wander at will and enjoy being able
to do just that. Guidance is
given for visiting the ponds.

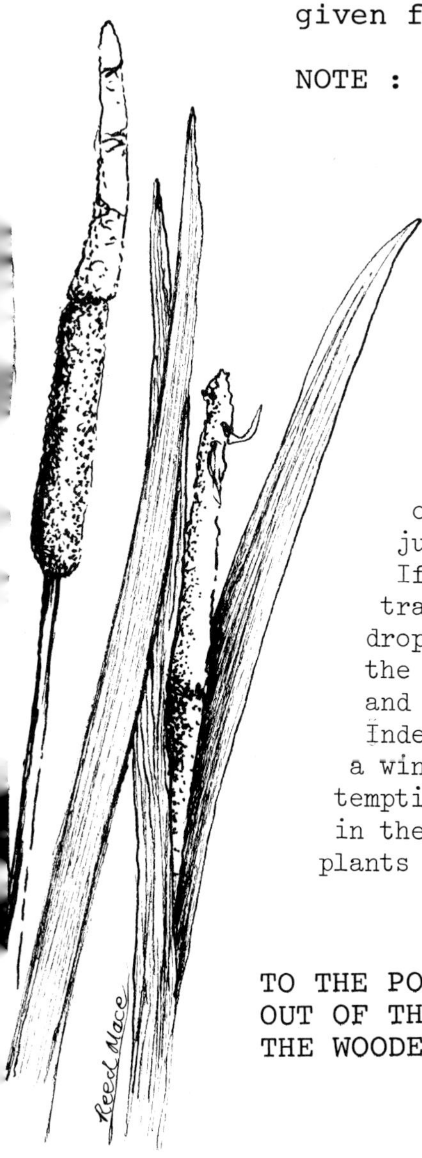

NOTE : The track down to the
pond is rough and stony
and not comfortable
for wheelchairs.
Pushchairs can be
pulled behind you!

THE SITE is a corner of
Chobham Common and of some
importance for retaining
open areas of ling.

Up on the higher areas of
this site it is very much
open heath, dominated by
just four species of plant.
If, however, you follow the
track down towards the pond you
drop down into a hollow where
the soils are deeper and richer
and the microclimate kinder.
Indeed it's a sheltered spot for
a winter walk when the sun is
tempting but the wind cold. Down
in the hollow the number of common
plants leaps up to twenty or so.

TO THE POND : FOLLOW THE MAIN TRACK
OUT OF THE CAR PARK AND IT LIES IN
THE WOODEN HOLLOW ON THE LEFT.

Reed Mace

Apart from the very
big pond there are
three others in the
trees at the end
nearest to the
car park.

The big pond
is often called
Gracious Pond,
after Gracious Pond
Road, but purists
point out that the real
Gracious Pond no longer
exists except as a wet area
administered as a nature
reserve (access restricted).
It is situated to the north of
this pond.

        The first Gracious Pond
was a valuable asset of Chertsey Abbey
back in the Middle Ages when it was used for fish farming
It is also said that the Abbey used these ponds too.
They were probably much smaller then as people can still
remember the present large pond being dredged out and
enlarged by steam engines, fifty years and more ago.

        The little ponds beside it are a regular feature
of old fisheries, used for raising baby fish until
large enough to fend for themselves in the big pond.
Each little pond here has its own ecology. The one
illustrated is deep and clear; the one beside it
becomes choked with water weeds; the third has all
but gone as the reed mace (illustrated) has invaded
and begun raising the soil level.

THERE IS A
PLEASANT WALK
RIGHT ROUND THE
LARGEST OF THE PONDS AND
INVITING SIDE PATHS THROUGH
THE WOODLAND AND OUT OVER
THE HEATHLAND.

The ponds, for some reason, do not attract such a
wide variety of waterfowl as the others in this
book but one never knows what will turn up. There's
always the simple pleasure of watching the moorhens
strutting over the lily leaves like retired naval
officers or the anglers landing massive tiddlers.

WEYBRIDGE : Tow-path and Back Streets
Distance : 1½ miles approx.

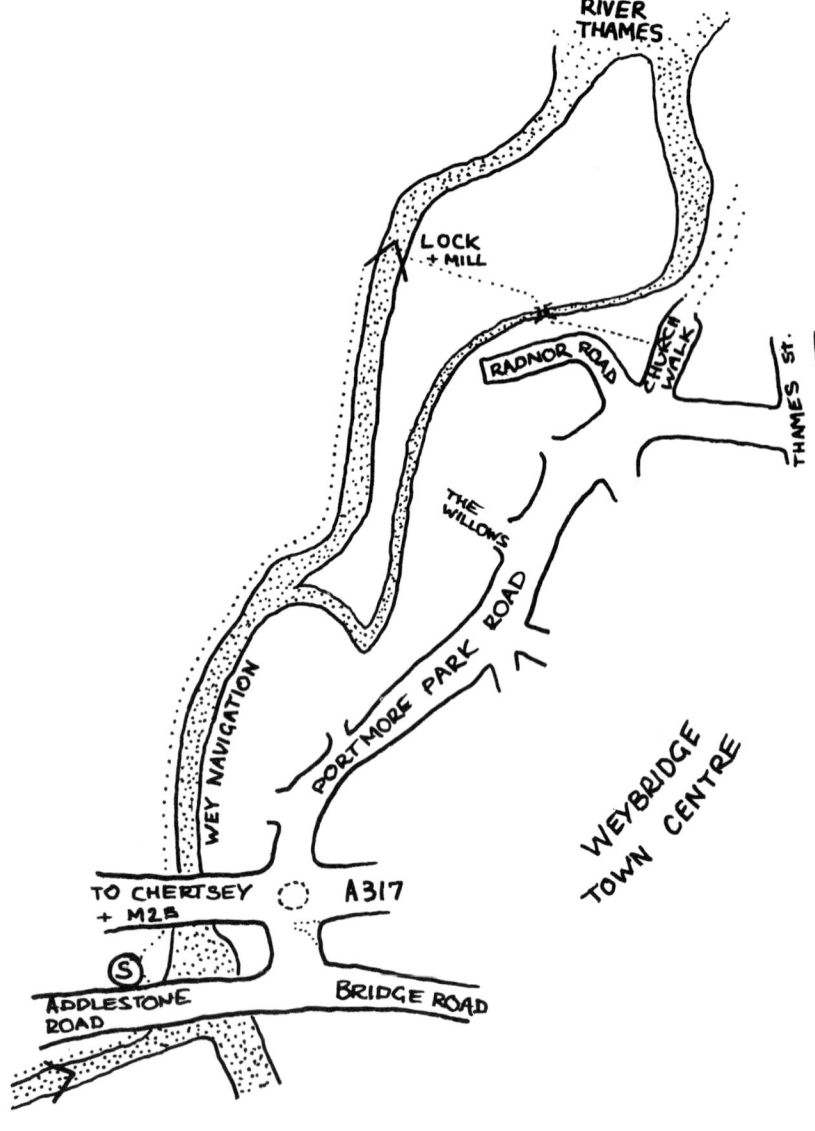

CAR PARKING : PORTMORE PARK ROAD USUALLY HAS
A SPACE.

BEGIN : SOUTHERN END OF PORTMORE PARK ROAD AT
JUNCTION WITH BRIDGE ROAD.

ON THE BRIDGE

Here the River Wey and the Wey Navigation rejoin and
brim into a wide pool with the old Weybridge Wharf on
the far side, once a busy with trade to and from the
London Docks.

JOIN THE TOW PATH from the end of the bridge. The
path now hugs the waterside, no longer passing behind
the building as shown in this sketch from 1980.

On the shoulder of land opposite the wharf is an old
upright roller post. This prevented the barge ropes
cutting the corner and, being a roller, saved them
from fraying as they were pulled round it.

FOLLOW THE TOWPATH DOWNSTREAM

You are leaving behind you the old ford through the
River Wey that was bridged in early medieval times
to give the settlement of Weybridge its name. The
present cast iron bridge is a fine example of a
factory product of 1865.

The path takes you through scenes rich
in trees and wildlife. It's difficul
to believe that a busy modern
town lies just over to your
right. Early on the route
there are old pollards
of ash and willow
from when the water-
way managers cut
back anything that
might overhang the river to impede the
traffic or the towing ropes. The off-cuts
or loppings became a source of firewood.

Some trees are clothed in ivy, providing shelter
for hibernating butterflies, like the brimstone, and
for small birds vulnerable to the cold, like the wren.
Woodcock (illustrated) have been flushed out of the
swampy ground beside here and kingfishers seen along
the side channels. It really is your lucky day if
you see either.

Meadowsweet decorates the wet places
with heads of foamy white flowers from June to
September; sweet when growing but pungent when it's
picked so it's been likened to young love ! Don't
pick it; everything along here is protected by the
National Trust. It was formerly called meadsweet
because since Anglo-Saxon times it was used to
flavour mead. It became a favourite strewing herb
for the floors of Elizabeth I's personal rooms and
so it may have been used in the nearby Oatlands
Palace.

You'll soon be approaching Whittet's Island but the
old mill site illustrated above may well have gone
before you walk this way as it is due for residential
redevelopment. That will end a tradition of milling
here that stretched back to the 1690s. Whittet was
the last miller.

CROSS THE RIVER BY THE BRIDGE

Here is the last of the 16 locks on the Wey before
it reaches the Thames and just a little further
downstream is a rare single-gate lock used to raise
the water level sufficiently for certain craft to be
able to clear the bottom cill of the main lock,
especially when the River Thames is running low.
The attractive lock cottage needed rebuilding but in so
doing the National Trust recreated its former appearance.
The old stables are preserved beside it.

FOLLOW PATH - CROSS ROAD - GO ON TO IRON IRON BRIDGE

single gate lock.

The bridge takes you over a side channel that helps to form Whittet's Island and which provides a vital overflow course from the main waterway, for all the water collected from the Wey's enormous catchment area gets funnelled down through here. Usually a good variety of birdlife can be watched about here.

CONTINUE to the houses of CHURCH PATH and TURN RIGHT.

Church Path is a delightful close space between mellowed 19th century housing that gives the best impression of the 'old Weybridge' that has largely gone elsewhere. The London yellow bricks and the blue Welsh slates show clearly the town's access to wider markets.

At the end, glance to the right, down Radnor Road for a different notion of 19th century housing: fine long terracing, now smartly refurbished.

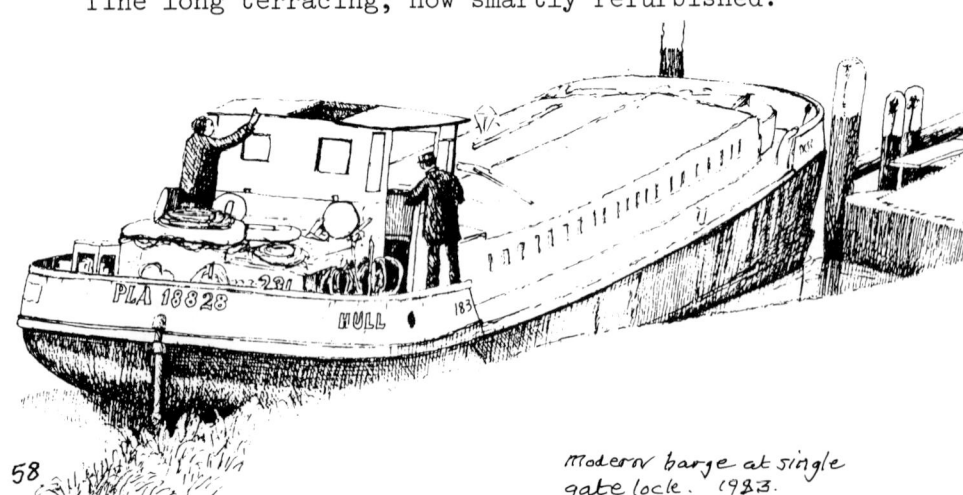

PLA 18828   HULL

modern barge at single gate lock. 1983.

TURN RIGHT INTO PORTMORE PARK ROAD

A glance left shows the road passing, in the distance, between a pair of white park gatepiers. They're 17th century, probably by Talman who rebuilt the park house in the lands of which this walk now progresses. It was owned by the 6th Duke of Norfolk, then King James II bought it for his mistress, Catherine Sedley, from who it descended to the Earls of Portmore who provided the name that has persisted.

In the 1890s the land was sold for housing. This new street was not mean but shows the influence of the Garden City concept, with sweeping curves between large gardens (overlook later infills), planted with fashionable evergreens. The most interesting of these is the large strawberry tree on the corner of Wey Road. You'll probably find it flowering and fruiting at the same time. Notice also, in places, the steep camber at the road edges, designed to help carriage horses push into their collars - in quieter Weybridge days.

WEYBRIDGE: New Line Ponds
Distance: 3 miles

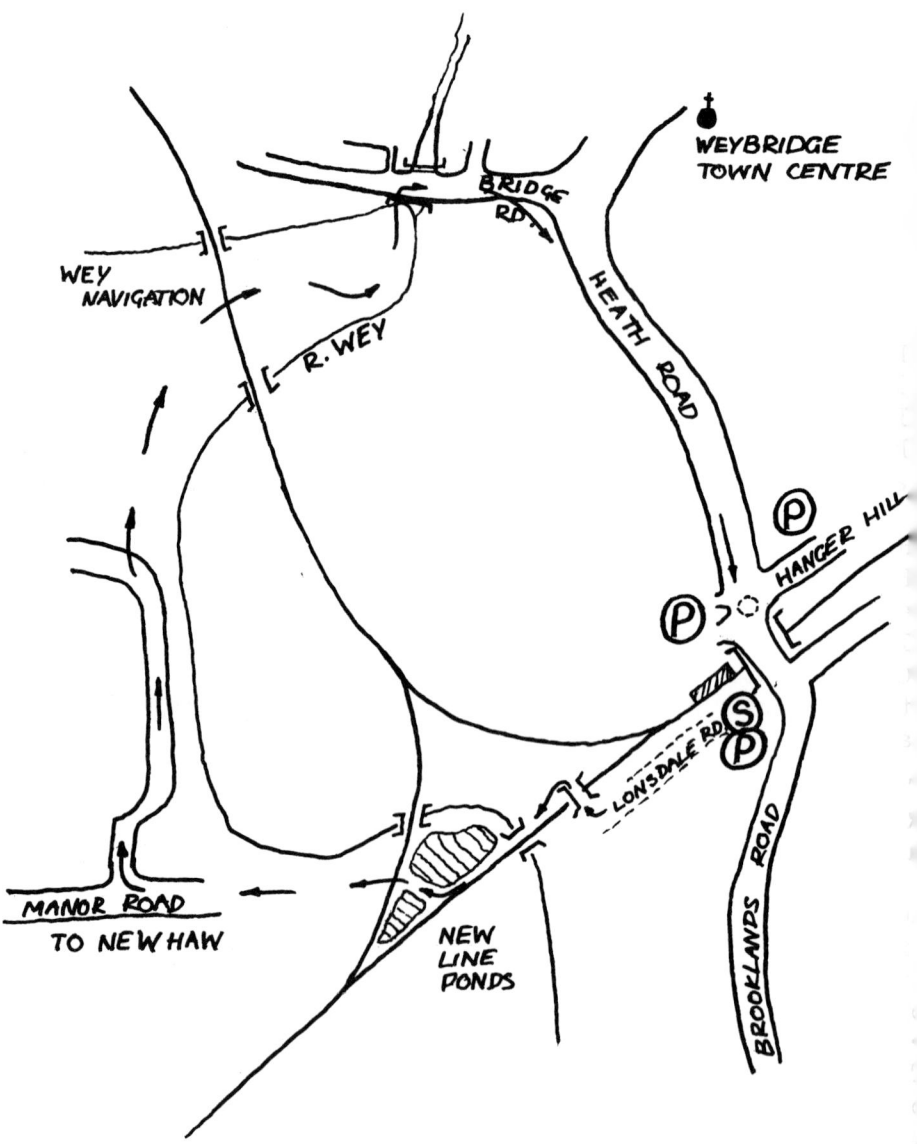

WEYBRIDGE TOWN CENTRE

BRIDGE RD.

WEY NAVIGATION

R. WEY

HEATH ROAD

HANGER HILL

LONSDALE RD.

MANOR ROAD
TO NEW HAW

NEW LINE PONDS

BROOKLANDS ROAD

CAR PARKING - Station Car Parks or
            side roads like
            Hanger Hill.

BEGIN - Car Park on east side
        of bridge, overlooking
        the station.

This was the first major railway
line in Surrey - 1838 - see date
on keystone of Buffers Restaurant
on the bridge for this was the
original station building. The
whole of the impressive cutting
here was of course dug by hand.

FOLLOW the path from the
lower end of car park - along
Lonsdale Road - RIGHT over the
bridge - LEFT along pavement
and down the track to the river.

Here the railway is carried over the
River Wey on the fine architecture of
a seven-arched brick viaduct. At water
level the brickwork is encrusted with
Great Scented Liverwort. Beyond it lies
the historic Brooklands Race Track and
air field.

FOLLOW the path round the pond and
RIGHT over the causeway between it
and a second swampy pond.

ere you can see how the roots of the Alder
rees raise the mud to a higher level to
reate fresh ground. The ponds were made
y extracting the gravel to build the
railway embankments - hence NEW LINE PONDS.
This is a good place for birds and insects
but the range of waterside plants is rather
limited. Rabbits and small rodents are also
plentiful.

Alder

CROSS the railway branch line. UNGUARDED
crossing so beware with children and dogs.

FOLLOW the path ahead. You'll pass through the
scrubby edges of open fields. Sometimes they've been
put down to pasture while in other years they're used
for rape, corn etc. Wild flowers are restricted to
those that thrive on dry sandy soils, such as the
coarse yellow Tansy. Water birds have now given way
to wrens and magpies in the scrub, crows and sometimes
lapwings out in the fields. Looking back right, the
chimneys are of Brooklands (Technical College),once
the home of Hugh Locke King who founded the Brooklands
race track, opened in 1907.

Path joins a track.
Continue ahead to
first turning RIGHT.
TURN RIGHT.
  (If you continue ahead
you reach New Haw Lock
and can follow the tow
path downstream to rejoin
this walk at Weybridge Lock;
extra mile approximately.

FOLLOW track up through
fields again. Where it
swings left follow the
field path under the line of
the power cables. The River Wey is
now over on the right.

CROSS railway embankment.
UNGUARDED crossing again.

This is the Chertsey branch line,
opened in 1848. The roofs over the
trees to the left are of Coxes Lock
Mill (1901/1906) closed for flour
milling in 1982 and now converted to
residential use as they are Listed.

Tansy

KEEP RIGHT of the
housing and you're
soon on their narrow
access road enjoying the
riverbank scenery and its
wildlife.

The land on your left is new.   There
was a flooded gravel pit here until a few
years ago.   It attracted much wildlife which has now been
displaced elsewhere but a few less common plants can still
be found from time to time; look out for Goat's Rue,
Galega officinalis.

TURN RIGHT at the road and stay on that road.

You may wish to explore a little here, where the Wey
Navigation and the River Wey join again at the great pool
with the former Weybridge wharf beyond.   This is part of
the alternative Weybridge walk in this book.

RIGHT at the green or cut diagonally across it to
the woods beside the road at the top.
Continue uphill and you'll reach the starting point.

GOING FURTHER

MUSEUMS

Further information on local history is provided by the museums at Chertsey, Egham, Kingston, Staines and Weybridge. They're listed in the local telephone directory so it's easy to check current opening times and special exhibitions. The same applies for specialised museums such as Brooklands and the Cobham Bus Museum.

LIBRARIES

Surrey County Library provides Information Centres at main branches like Weybridge and Woking. The greatest collection of printed material is housed in the Local Studies Library on the top floor of Guildford Library in North Street.

ORGANISATIONS concerned with Local History and Natural History

N.W.Surrey is well covered by these. Libraries and Museums can usually tell you whom to contact. Some Local History Societies, such as Send and Ripley, have a natural history section. Other organisations, like the Chertsey Society and the Cultural Section of New Haw Community Association, cater for countryside concerns in their activities.

ACTIVITIES
See local press for special events.

CHANGES
Please notify the publishers of any changes you find that concern the contents of this book.